WHY BE A CATHOLIC?

The 1978 Albany Forum

Edited by
Brennan Hill, Ph.D.
Mary Reed Newland

uɾb

Wm. C. Brown Company Publishers
Dubuque, Iowa

Craig M. Brown—Cover and Design

ISBN 0-697-01713-3

CONTENTS

ANSWERING THE QUESTION......67

SUMMARY............................85

PARTICIPANTS

Dr. Monika Hellwig, author and educator, is a Professor of Theology at Georgetown University.

Ms. Gertrude Morris is the Director of Culture and Worship for the National Office of Black Catholics in Washington, DC.

Rev. Philip Murnion is Chairman of the Catholic Committee on Urban Ministry.

Rev. David Murphy, O. Carm., is Campus Minister and theology instructor at St. Mary's College, Notre Dame.

Dr. David O'Brien is Professor of Church History at Stonehill College and Director of the Stonehill Institute of Justice and Peace.

Rev. Antonio Stevens-Arroyo, C.P., is Executive Director of the Research Center for Evangelization and Ministry.

Rev. Robley Whitson, theologian, is President of the United Institute, Bethlehem, Connecticut.

EDITORS

Brennan Hill, Ph.d., educator and author on the staff of the Office of Religious Education for the Diocese of Albany.

Mary Reed Newland, educator and author on the staff of the Office of Religious Education for the Diocese of Albany.

Introduction

In our work with Catholics in the diocese of Albany and in other parts of the U.S. and Canada we hear one question constantly being asked—"Why be a Catholic?" Some ask the question from a position of indifference. Either they once were Catholics and now feel that the Church has little to offer them, or they have never been Catholics and see no rhyme or reason for belonging to such an organization. Others ask the question from a posture of alienation. They were once Catholics, but because of some incident or teaching have now dropped out of the Church. Still others pose the question in the context of an honest search for their own Catholic identity. The Church which they knew has changed so much. Moreover, a great deal of recognition has been given to the validity of other churches and faiths. So many Catholics find themselves faced with the challenge of digging into the roots of their Catholic faith, seeking for sound reasons and motives for renewing their Catholic commitment. They can no longer regard the Church as the only path to salvation. They can no longer mechanically cling to a religious routine uniform among Catholics. There is no longer a single identifiable Catholic culture to support their faith. They must now formulate their own personal commitment, deciding where they stand in the community vis-a-vis the institutional Church.

Given the importance of this question, we thought it would be useful to devote the second Albany Forum to a discussion on the topic of "Why be a Catholic?" We invited a cross section of participants to discuss the question with representatives from our sponsors, Wm. C. Brown Company and Peter Li, Inc., and with the members of our religious education staff. The selected participants were: Dr. Monika Hellwig, Professor at Georgetown University; Ms. Gertrude Morris, Director of Culture and Worship for the National Office of Black Catholics; Dr. David O'Brien, Director of the Stonehill Institute of Justice and Peace; Rev. David Murphy, Campus Minister and theology instructor at St. Mary's College, Notre Dame; Rev. Robley Whitson, President of the United Institute; Rev. Philip Murnion, Chairman of the Catholic Committee on Urban Ministry; and Rev. Antonio Stevens-Arroyo, C.P., the Executive Director of the Research Center for Evangelization and Ministry, CEMI.

part one:

BACKGROUND
FOR
DISCUSSION

The Participants' Experience of the Question

We began the forum by asking the participants to relate the circumstances wherein they had met the question "Why be a Catholic?" and to suggest what could be done in the discussion to serve the question.

Gertrude Morris represented the point of view of blacks when she said that many blacks find it incongruous that Catholics proclaim the gospel of Jesus and yet are often racists. Such a posture tends to ruin Catholic credibility for blacks. She added that since, in her experience, the majority of black Catholics are converts, they have already made a personal commitment and are seldom merely nominal Catholics. One pattern she found in her inquiry among black Catholics, and this seems to be true across racial lines, is that people tend to have lofty reasons for their own personal commitment to Catholicism, but tend to see others as having very mundane and mechanical reasons.

Dr. Monica Hellwig, who has a varied religious background that includes Jewish as well as Protestant elements, said that she found Catholicism a satisfying and good place to be. She was surprised to discover when she came to Georgetown that many of her colleagues had a sense of embarrassment about their own Catholicism. They tended to down play the Catholic tradition and considered Protestant theology to be much more attractive. Dr. Hellwig believes that Catholics very often sell themselves short and become apologetic regarding their own tradition, which is enormously rich. She finds it ironic that Catholic universities are often hesitant to offer courses on Catholicism, when frequently youth have a genuine interest in the Catholic tradition. In her experience in teaching the Catholic tradition, however, she has always found it important to distinguish between the essential specifics and those which are accidental. She concentrates on the central themes of doctrine, and gives much attention to how these themes can be best presented today.

Fr. Stevens-Arroyo approaches the question of "Why be a Catholic?" from the perspective of Third World liberation theology. He was raised as if he were an Irish Catholic, but as an adolescent discovered his Puerto Rican heritage. He believes that he was ordained at a propitious time when both the Church and its people were developing a new self-consciousness. The old identity of the Church was changing and a new age of renewal was opening. At the same time, Hispanic people were leaving behind the identity given them by capitalistic colonialism and emerging with a fresh new identity, one that is rooted in the past Hispanic traditions and often mixed with socialism and liberation theology.

David O'Brien pointed out that in the past the reasons for being Catholic were largely cultural, and, when articulated, were presented as apologetics. Now the reasons spring from a more personal point of view. We are not as interested in building up the pride of the group or defending ourselves as we are in formulating the terms of our own personal commitment within a pluralistic Church. Dr. O'Brien added that many parents are moved to search for explicit reasons to be

Catholic because their youngsters no longer accept the former reasons and are able to move freely in and out of other religions. A parent whose child has become a Baptist or a Buddhist has to go back and look seriously at Catholicism's validity.

Fr. Philip Murnion pointed to two current phenomena that have sharpened the question "Why be a Catholic?" First of all, the Second Vatican Council declared that social ministry was constitutive of the Church's mission. The Catholic identity now has to include dedication to social justice and peace, and the Church must see itself as a servant to the needs of the world. As a result there is a call for coherence between Catholic belief and action. Once it is recognized that the message within the community has to overflow in service, the question arises as to what is distinctive about

Catholic social action, and ministry enters the Catholic identity question.

Ecumenism is the second phenomenon that has helped Catholics focus on their own tradition. According to Fr. Murnion, effective ecumenical dialogue requires Catholics to return to their roots and have a clearer notion of their own identity. Vagueness about Catholic traditions is certainly no position from which to speak to other churches or faiths.

Fr. David Murphy looks to his pastoral experience and finds that many Catholics have gone to the periphery of the Church. They have not replaced their past religious way of life with anything, and find themselves in a religious vacuum. They often keep up the appearances of being Catholic, but have no depth of commitment nor concern for where the Church is going. The young people he encounters in university teaching are often quite illiterate in their Catholic faith. They tend to simply gather the required credits in theology rather mechanically, and see these courses as the end of religious thinking. Even though they may be searching for religious roots, they are turning less and less to the Church for guidance or inspiration.

Fr. Robley Whitson finds that so often we answer the question "Why be a Catholic?" autobiographically, but when it comes to looking at the *catholic substance* we are at a loss. He was eager to see this discussion tease out the substantive characteristics of Catholicism, the objective positions upon which all Catholics can agree.

Fr. Whitson related a story from his great-grand-parents who were Swedenborgians. The great-grand-father reputedly appeared to his wife and all the family after his death and confirmed the final truths of their religious beliefs. When her children became Catholics, his wife was asked how this could be in view of the apparition of the grandfather. Her delightfully ecumenical answer was: "My husband showed us that Swedenborgianism is true. My children are finding out what else might be true." This interesting background has always inclined Whitson to think in a nonsectarian fashion and to be open to discover truth in other religions. It is his conviction that Catholic ecumenical dialogue must broaden beyond the mainline Protestant churches and be open to groups like Christian Scientists and Swedenborgians. In their search for religious truth, Catholics are preparing a future Catholicism that will have to consider scientific technology and a wide variety of religious lifestyles.

The Basic Elements of Catholicism

Any attempt to answer the question "Why be a Catholic?" must first involve establishing the basic elements of Catholicism. What are those elements which are essential to the Catholic faith? And, of course, such a search is difficult since Christianity has had major divisions since the time of the separation of the Orthodox and the tragic breakup during the Reformation. As Fr. Stevens-Arroyo put it: "When does Catholicism actually begin—with Jesus?—at the time of the great schism?—at the Reformation? The divisions of Christianity make it extremely difficult to establish elements which are uniquely Roman Catholic.

Even though one could proceed from a broader base of Christianity and its essentials, this discussion confined itself to the particularities of Roman Catholicism. What is different about Catholicism? While Ms. Morris cautioned us not to use comparisons which would denigrate other churches, we had to proceed realistically, knowing that we do hold positions opposing those of other religions and churches. As Fr. Whitson put it, we can't be so conciliatory that we can't take clear stands.

Rather courageously, Dr. Hellwig proposed a method for identifying these Catholic elements. She pointed out that there are three approaches to defining Catholicism. First, there is the descriptive account, such as we have in cultural anthropology. Here one looks at the customs and artifacts which Catholics have left behind in their long history. Second, there is the definitive account of Catholicism from outside observation. From this detached position, one lists the objective characteristics which constitute the Catholic religion. Finally, and this is the approach she intends to follow, there is the self-definitive way, wherein the people inside the Church ask normative questions regarding what is critical to the faith and cite traditions which they consider must be transmitted.

Using the self-definitive method, Dr. Hellwig offered five distinguishing features of Roman Catholicism, features through which Catholics can distinguish themselves from other faith persuasions.

1. *The sacramental principle.* Catholics celebrate sacraments, because they have the conviction that the presence of God is mediated through concrete ritual

Dr. Monica Hellwig offered five distinguishing features of Roman Catholicism, features through which Catholics can distinguish themselves from the other persuasions. The five features are: the sacramental principle; the thrust toward universality; an appreciation of the accumulative wisdom of the past; a commitment to the reasonableness of faith; and a corporate response. Dr. Hellwig sees the five elements as both an ideal and a reality.

symbols and events which they as a community constitute. Catholics believe that as Church they can actually create meeting places with God.

2. *A thrust toward universality.* Catholicism by its very nature is not an exclusive or an elitist religion. It is open to participation by all kinds of peoples and cultures throughout the world. We might add here how magnificantly this was brought out at the recent funerals and installations in Rome.

3. *An appreciation of the accumulative wisdom of the past.* Catholics honor tradition, and place great value in passing on tradition in an original purity that is adopted to the current time.

4. *A commitment to the reasonableness of the faith.* The Church has always held that the faith can be approached with reason and reflection. It encourages theology and critical thinking. The faith always stands open to questioning and encourages a serious search for deeper understanding.

5. *A corporate response.* Catholic spirituality is not simply a matter of one person with a bible, but involves membership in a community with a unique lifestyle that witnesses to the presence of God in the human community.

Dr. Hellwig's format provided an excellent context for a discussion of the essentials of Catholicism, and the reaction of the group was varied. Fr. Murnion found these "charmingly traditional" in the good sense. We might have described the Church before Vatican II in similar fashion, but we would have used different terminology, such as "the marks" of the Church. He suggested, however, that perhaps the Church's consciousness had developed in such a way over the past few decades that the norms of Catholicism have really changed. He proposed that we have to broaden the notion of "sacramental" to include the symbolic; consider pluralism as the current phrasing of "universality"; regard historicity as a broader conception than "tradition"; consider the persuasiveness of faith as involving more than "reasonableness"; and focus on the communitarian character of the Church rather than its corporate character. Dr. Hellwig granted that the norms had been modified and reinterpreted, but she would not grant that they have changed. There has always been a strong thread of continuity in the Church.

Reinterpretation of the corporate nature of the Church has obviously taken place. Mary Newland observed that in the past the Church was highly institutionized and the corporate stance was closed and defensive. Today the accent is on community and personhood, with an openness to the world and other religions. Monica Hellwig added that in the past the papacy and authority were central in corporate life, whereas in the contemporary Church both these factors are important, but not central.

Fr. Murphy inquired as to whether these five elements are simply desiderata (what the Church wants to have) or actually part of the Catholic experience. Couldn't it be said that these elements are also found in such churches as the Episcopalian and Lutheran?

Dr. Hellwig answered that these elements are both an ideal and a reality. She finds a solid foundation for all five elements in Catholicism, yet she is willing to concede that throughout its history the Church has betrayed some of these elements. As for the presence of these elements in other faiths, she perceives them as having only a partial claim to all five. The Episcopalian and Lutheran churches, she contends, lack a universal thrust.

Fr. Whitson pointed up a valuable clarification regarding these norms. These norms are so entrenched in Catholic tradition that if Catholics don't follow them, they are embarrassed. For instance, if people are excluded from the Church community because of race or social status, we have to admit that we are falling short of gospel teaching. If we neglect the sacramental life, our commitment to Catholicism is inadequate. We have stated positions and these stand as a judgment on how we live.

Dr. Hellwig developed this further by stating that Catholicism follows a constitutional model in that it has a corpus of statements which continually stands as normative. We can constantly return to these positions for renewal of self-evaluation. It is within these constitutional formulations that Catholics can discover the essential elements of their identity.

Dr. O'Brien picked up this constitutional notion and pointed out that by way of comparison the Constitution of the United States only makes sense if it is part of the continuing life of this country. Likewise, the Church can't let its constitutional elements freeze or be a basis for self-justification and imperilialism. The community must continually redefine itself in terms of its life within and its relationships to other faiths.

Fr. Stevens-Arroyo addressed the area of sacramentality. If this is a basic element, need it be exercised in the present system of clericalism? Can't sacramentality be carried out by the people? Dr. Hellwig cited instances of folk Catholicism and rituals carried out during times of persecution to establish that clericalism is not essential to sacramentality.

As for the thrust toward universality, Fr. Stevens-Arroyo cautioned that this should not imply imperialism, or colonialism, on the part of the mission Church. Moreover, "corporateness," when referring to the communal dimension, should not imply hierarchical structure or elitism. Vatican II has pointed up the equality that exists among members of the Church.

Dr. O'Brien tried to put all five elements of Catholicism into historical perspective. These Catholic elements are derived from a reflection on Roman Catholic history. He believes, however, that we must go beyond this context and look at other histories, which perhaps have preserved elements lost in Catholicism. Moreover, we must look into the living experience of Catholicism as an experience which reaches into the future. That which is essential is that which will help us build the future. Fr. Whitson agreed and added that each element of Catholicism must be tested out in terms of future relevancy. We are, after all, building a Church that will reach into the next millennium. What we establish as essential must be able to speak to coming generations.

At this point in the discussion Fr. Murnion stated that he found these five elements too restrictive and limiting. In his mind, they tended to set up boundaries determining who is in and who is out. They echo elements of the establishment. It is his conviction that the Church's self-consciousness has so radically changed in our time that there must be new categories. Once we grant that the Church is a mystery, we cannot continue to define it in such definite terms.

Dr. Hellwig replied that no matter how much the Church changes, self-identification does not start in the here and now. Catholics belong to a tradition older and larger than the present community, and the essentials must have a continuity throughout history.

The Catholic Identity

The discussion turned its attention to the Catholic identity. It appears that many Catholics today are having difficulty with identity. There seems to be such a plurality, even within the Church itself, that it becomes hard to place oneself in the community.

Mary Newland observed that the identity problem comes in a garden variety. In the inner city there are many unchurched Catholics who may have their own style of religiosity, but have little or no association with parish or diocesan activity. Then, there are many of our Catholic youth who have received little religious information or experience, and maintain only a vague and tenuous Catholic identity. Finally, the inner city unchurched and the youth view the Church quite differently from many of the middle class, who simply feel that they have outgrown the Church. Ms. Newland warned against making snap judgments about people's commitment to the Church. She has experienced young people as apparently outside the Church, only to discover that they have their own unique way of being Catholic. There exists such a plurality of ways to be a Catholic today that people can't be put in tight little boxes.

Fr. Murphy suggested that Catholic identity is formulated by relating to the essential elements and symbols of the faith. The way a person views God, Trinity, creation, redemption, sacraments, and so on, determines identity. Our youth often have such a vague notion of the Catholic symbol system that their church identity is vague. Heaven is a place in the sky, Mass a superstitious ritual, and sin a legal defect. To counteract this distortion of symbols, the Church must reinterpret the symbols in such a way that they speak to people's lives. At that point the acceptance of Catholic elements and the construction of a Catholic identity becomes feasible.

Fr. Murnion agreed that changing models of belief are affecting Catholic identity. People are changing their images of God and this affects their thinking about the Church, the sacraments, and their personal spirituality. The more comfortable people are with God, sharing His life, the more free they feel to make their own religious decisions and use their gifts in ministry.

The freezing of Catholic symbols seems to be a major obstacle in establishing identity in the Church, according to Fr. Whitson. To remain truly orthodox the Church must remain dynamic in its symbol system. It is actually heretical to absolutize anything other than God or to allow our symbols themselves to substitute for the mystery they reveal. Fr. Stevens-Arroyo added that when we adore symbols of God we lose contact with genuine faith and authentic practice of faith. Moreover, our youth must have the faith first before we deal with the symbol system. Dr. Hellwig responded that reinterpreting these symbols for our alienated youth, however, is not a lost enterprise. Symbols can build up a context and an atmosphere for the acceptance of the gift of faith. Even without faith, symbols can touch human chords and dispose youth toward the faith. Fr. Whitson agreed and cited an example in which a young girl was moved to faith in God by witnessing the rich symbolism in a Jewish Orthodox service. Ancient symbols, often long forgotten, can be restored and have the power to move people to faith.

It was pointed out by Dr. O'Brien how typically American it is to abandon old symbols and construct new ones. The immigrant move to the New World was characterized by this attitude. But Catholics must remember the importance of historical memory and the immense value of continuing traditions; Christianity needs to recall concrete historical events and a specific historic person. At present the Third World stands in danger of breaking with universal (Catholic) traditions because of the thrust to reinterpret Christian symbols in terms of local culture. This danger of extreme localization was cited by Paul VI after the Synod on Evangelization. Catholics have an obligation to the past as well as the present, and there is always a mutual responsibility among Church communities throughout the world to be faithful to the Catholic traditions. This is not to say that we can manipulate our symbols in order to stifle other cultures and other religions. The balance between creative accommodation to diverse cultures and true universality is always hard to maintain.

Fr. Whitson recommended that our symbols be future oriented. Conservatives tend to stay with the past and show little concern for the future. It is true that there is a power within ancient symbols, such as those preserved by the Greek Orthodox, but sooner or later the future catches up with churches who persistently live in the past.

Fr. Murphy observed that Catholic identity has been seriously challenged by the cultural and religious "explosion" that has gone on all around us. He likened

Rev. Antonio Stevens—Arroyo, C.P. (left), Rev. Robley Whitson, (right).

the experience to one of standing on the edge of a swift-moving stream. Some remain on shore, clinging to the past and refusing to enter the currents. Others jump into the currents recklessly and are tossed here and there aimlessly. He recommends carefully entering the movement of the water, trusting oneself to the mystery of God's unfolding plan.

Secularization was also cited as a factor in the Catholic identity crisis. The Church has been ambiguous about human progress, and yet the contemporary Catholic is caught up in the sweep of modern progress. Dr. Hellwig pointed out that faith is often in conflict with secularization, which ignores the radical positions of Christian teaching.

Fr. Stevens-Arroyo pointed out that secularization ignores the significance of Jesus. Jesus is the only sacrament of Christianity. Centered in him we are able to enter into human progress with a center and a goal. It is Jesus who reveals the reality of a life dedicated to love. He sets the standard for a life style of genuine growth and progress.

Fr. Whitson developed this idea further. Jesus is central in the Catholic identity as the only adequate image of God and human life. In him we discover the meaning of human existence. All our other images are limited and tentative and can find their meaning only in relation to Jesus. Papacy, sacraments, priesthood, all these must be derived from Jesus and his significance.

Cultural Catholic vs. Believing Catholic

This portion of the discussion was begun by Gertrude Morris who moved the group by saying: "The test of a believing Catholic is whether he or she would be willing to die for the faith." Being a cultural Catholic is too much like belonging to a club. The believing Catholic acknowledges that if one isn't willing to die for the faith, then one isn't willing to live for it. This doesn't necessarily mean physical death, but certainly includes a death to self and to certain comforts.

Dr. Hellwig remarked that both the terms *cultural* and *believing* held a wide variety of meanings and that there should be a continuum involved here. She would hope that all who called themselves members of the Church would be moving along such a continuum from their Catholic cultural heritage to a personal commitment. This is the normal maturation process within the Church and we should not be too hasty in sorting people out as cultural or believing. The Church has never been successful at trying to be a purist organization that excludes certain types of people. *Cultural Catholic* need not refer to one who is institutionally acceptable, but should refer to one who has made a personal commitment. She cautions against dividing people into cultural vs. believing Catholics; everyone is somehow on a continuum between the two positions.

Fr. Whitson was quite wary of the distinction between cultural and believing Catholics. The cultural involves much more than mere mechanical commitment, and personal belief naturally integrates much of the cultural. He cited a study that Gordon Allport did for B'nai B'rith to analyse the source of postwar and anti-Semitism. The study revealed that it is extremely difficult to accurately sort out religious motivation. It is wrong, according to Fr. Whitson, to try to sort people out on the basis of a judgment about their religious commitment. Therefore, the Church cannot stand in judgment of who is in and who is out, but must always give individuals the benefit of the doubt regarding their religious sincerity.

The term *believing Catholic* was not adequate for Fr. Murphy to ascertain real commitment to Catholicism. He pointed out that most Catholics, no matter what their relationship to the Church, would describe themselves as believers. He would like to introduce the term *prophetic Catholic* to describe those who act out of their faith and give visible witness to gospel teaching. It is his conviction that many *believing Catholics* take little or no prophetic positions as a result of their beliefs.

Dr. O'Brien observed that religious education at its worst is designed to browbeat cultural Catholics into becoming believing Catholics. At its best, religious education encourages people to be confident and articulate in their beliefs and allows freedom for acceptance of the gift of faith. He too warned about hasty judgments. People whom we might easily classify as merely cultural Catholics often are just not able to articulate what is in reality a deep commitment to the faith.

According to Dr. O'Brien, there should be definite

boundaries within the community. We should call each other to an accounting, and in extreme cases excommunication might be the only alternative. Without some kinds of parameters and norms there can be no genuine Catholic identity. Dr. Hellwig agreed that there should be doctrinal boundaries, but found it difficult to see how moral boundaries could be established. To do the latter would mean judging people. She accepts a principle of exclusion, but is quite wary as to how it would be applied, especially in light of the mistakes that were made toward the divorced. Fr. Whitson added that it is not proper to say that we don't care how people believe, but how do we deal with those who depart from the norm if we are still to be true to the gospel? He expressed difficulty with identifying practice or moral behavior with Catholic commitment. Moral status is not a good criterion for membership, since we are a community of sinners. Sin doesn't necessarily imply disbelief.

Fr. Stevens-Arroyo holds that what primarily determines the genuine Catholic identity is the practice of the faith, the carrying out of a loving life-style. The cultural aspect of the faith did not exist in the beginning, and today becomes less and less important. Commitment today is understood to be more a prophetic stance than commitment to an institution or a set of symbols. Catholics do not have a uniform culture of their own. Moreover, they often find themselves in opposition to the oppression, hatred and prejudice that exists in their contemporary culture. Catholic culture as such is dying out. The official institutional positions are no longer acceptable and the old structured Church is on the wane. Unstructured commitment, such as we so often find in charismatics and Third World activists, is growing. At present we are abandoning older Catholic forms and taking on new forms that are highly influenced by contemporary society. So we don't want to pass on a Catholic identity that is embracing dying institutional forms, and a cultural form of life that is archaic.

Dr. O'Brien pointed out the importance of what he calls the Catholic subculture. Every community creates customs and a way of life that sustains its present members and attracts new ones. Many people are attracted to parish social life and events like church suppers. There is nothing wrong with these activities, as long as down the road participation in social events leads them to participate in the life of faith. Such participation is distinct from participation in a cultural Catholicism—for example, American Catholicism—wherein church members get trapped in a process of secularization that is counter to gospel values.

The question arose concerning the validity of Rahner's description of the *diaspora* Church of the future. Will the Church of the future in fact be a "little flock" as distinct from vast numbers of nominal Catholics? Dr. Hellwig did not see the contemporary scene revealing the development of such a "little flock." Nor did Fr. Whitson agree that the labeling of many members of the Church as nominal Catholic is a realistic description of the Church today or in the future.

Fr. Stevens-Arroyo agrees with Rahner that the age of Christendom is over. If there is to be a cultural Catholicism now it will involve dialogue with other ideologies such as Communism. He said this new culture will oppose the old institutional structures which often opposed freedom, and will incorporate the liberation notions from movements such as socialism. He pointed out the phenomenon in Cuba, where Catholics are discovering the State dealing with many social needs so that the Church there must reflect on what it uniquely brings to these arenas of social justice.

Fr. Murnion said that Catholic cultural identity will have to look not only at its doctrinal positions but also its social positions. Has the Church been an agent of change in areas of civil rights, human rights, and social justice? He believes that Catholicism has a unique capacity for international interdependence and that it can offer the world a model for global community concern.

part one:
Discussion Questions

1. Discuss the five features of Catholicism proposed by Dr. Hellwig. Would you accept them as the distinguishing characteristics of Catholicism? Would you propose any other characteristics?

2. Discuss Rahner's description of the *diaspora* Church. Do you think it accurately describes the direction in which the Church is moving?

3. Dr. Hellwig noted that it surprised her to find that some U.S. Catholics were embarrassed to be Catholic. Have you ever experienced this embarrassment? Why do you think some people are embarrassed by their Catholic identity?

4. In the Introduction the editors note that many people feel that the Church has little to offer them. How do you feel about what the Church has to offer?

5. Fr. Murnion stated that the Vatican II Church has associated itself with social justice and peace. Are the Church and social justice linked in your mind? Can you describe areas in which your local Church is involved with peace and social justice?

6. Mary Newland observed that many middle-class people feel that they have outgrown the Church. What do you think they mean by that?

7. What would you describe as the essential or basic elements in your own identity as a Catholic?

part two:

THE
CATHOLIC
IN
AMERICA

American Catholicism

Dr. David O'Brien opened the discussion on American Catholicism by briefly sketching the historical background of the hierarchy. The American bishops in the nineteenth century had two fundamental needs: (1) to maintain their own authority and prevent ethical and cultural diversity from fragmenting the American church; and (2) to keep Rome, which did not understand the pastoral requirements of the American church, at arm's length.

Sometime between the Third Plenary Council of Baltimore in 1884 and World War I, there was a breakdown of that unity, and individual bishops began to consider Rome, rather than the American church, as the focus of their allegiance. This resulted from three factors: (1) initiatives by Rome designed to bring the American church, once a missionary church but now getting larger and more significant, within the discipline of the newly centralized church of Vatican I being institutionalized by Leo XIII; (2) divisions within the American hierarchy itself. The earlier bishops had been aware that division was dangerous because it would allow Rome to move in, but as American liberals began to emerge on the Catholic scene after 1884, both liberals and conservatives had recourse to Rome to win their points (which was a big mistake); (3) a new generation of bishops found that using Roman authority, rather than the fragile consensus of the American hierarchy, was a surer way of establishing and maintaining their own authority in their own dioceses than reliance on episcopal collegiality.

The end result was a Roman dominated church, the key to which was the control of seminary training, the Romanization of theology, the condemnation of the Modernist crisis, and the firming up of orthodoxy. After the death of Cardinal Gibbons, Rome saw to it that there were no more cardinals in Baltimore, and the attempt to make Catholic University the cultural and intellectual center of the American church failed.

A member of the Albany staff asked if the experience of the Albany diocese in being consulted on the choice of its new bishop was significant of some Roman policy change. Philip Murnion felt that question raised another: Should there be an apostolic delegate at all to prevent Rome's dealing with the American hierarchy in a collective sense? Dr. O'Brien believed that an indication of a change in policy would be confirmed if the same process were observable in the choosing of bishops for the six or eight key dioceses in the country. After his experience with the Call to Action*, it seemed clear that national efforts as such are heavily dependent upon a limited number of members of the hierarchy. He reflected that the history of the National Catholic Welfare Conference is the history of a small group of bishops who continue to take an interest in a national organization for the American bishops and who are

_____

*The "Call to Action" assembly was held October 21–23, 1976, in Detroit, Michigan, under the auspices of the National Conference of Catholic Bishops. The assembly contributed to the development of a five year plan of social action for the Church in the United States. The plan is also known as the "Call to Action."

responsible for the good things it does, but who also have to be careful not to step on toes.

Dr. O'Brien pointed out that the bishops, in formulating their response to the Call to Action, took pains to emphasize their responsibilities for maintaining and strengthening of the teachings of Rome. An amendment to this statement, stating that it was also the responsibility of the bishops to articulate to the universal church the pastoral needs of the American church was introduced, but was defeated! This seemed to indicate that, unlike the African bishops and the South American bishops, the bishops of the United States do not feel pressed to enter into dialogue with Rome about the needs of their own church.

Americans Seeking Community

Dr. O'Brien went on to say that the issues which engage the theologians, whose concern is the order of the Church, and the activists, who are concerned with what the Church does, are often far removed from the people's concerns. He recalled that the very goal of the bicentennial consultations, under the auspices of the hierarchy, was an effort to strengthen the Church's social ministries. However, one of the conclusions of the Call to Action was that the priority of U.S. Catholics was not the Church's work or its belief, but its existence as a community. The working paper on Church said that the most notable conclusion of the Call to Action was the degree to which the participants had internalized the notion of church-as-community, as People of God, and used this image to measure the well-being and vitality of the local church and to suggest needed reforms.

The reality of the American Catholic community, he continued, is itself problematic and cannot be taken for granted. The existence of that community is undeniably for proclamation and service, but it is the fostering of the community that is the real priority of the people at the moment, rather than the explicit work the church does or even the explicit proclamation of its message. To be able to find a community of affirmation and care—in which certain vital concerns such as family needs and the transmission of Christian values are provided for—is, he believes, the popular priority in the American Church.

Dr. David O'Brien points out that the reality of the American Catholic community is itself problematic and cannot be taken for granted. The popular priority in the American Church, he believes, is to be able to find a community of affirmation and care.

Advocacy for American Catholics

The machinery exists whereby a dynamic could be created to surface needs of American Catholics, Dr. O'Brien pointed out. The United States Catholic Conference Advisory Council is something which ought to be consulted and appealed to more from the local level, and a national lay organization could, among other things, open up this channel for the people. He cited the Good Shepherd parish case, in Alexandria, Virginia (wherein the people of a parish attempted to protest the action of their pastor), as a tragic example of how the people have nowhere to appeal other than to Rome.

Asked if this situation would eventually force people on the local level to improvise solutions without leadership, it was Dr. O'Brien's opinion that one or two key bishops in the larger dioceses would make an enormous difference. He felt that one of the tragedies in recent years was the blackballing of talented clergy with gifts for leadership because of the stand they took on *Humanae Vitae.*

Fr. Murnion felt that one of the ambiguities with respect to the USCC was the bishops' tentative approach to the activities and positions of their own organization. Even so, it has built up a momentum that could promise much for the future. There are good staff people in key positions, and some key bishops have given the USCC credibility and stature by committing themselves to it. These factors could make an enormous difference. Pope John XXIII was an example of how one figure catches a movement and makes a difference. Hopefully this same thing could happen in the American church.

What issues, it was asked, might the American bishops support and fight for as specifically American Catholic needs? Dr. O'Brien pointed out that the American bishops have united to fight for changes in some of the marriage norms in the American church—which simply confirms the belief that in order for the bishops to take a clear stand, there must be a visible need. Perhaps the problem, he said, is that the needs are not clearly visible to them. This situation says something about the need for American Catholic laymen to continue to surface the crucial issues in order that the bishops do see them.

Ms. Gertrude Morris pointed out that as a black she would not recommend that anyone want to be on the bottom of the heap, but that being there has one advantage: one is challenged to do big things. When the challenge disappears, so does a certain vitality. The African bishops have it, and many South American bishops, but the Americans seem to have lost that impetus. Perhaps one of the prices to be paid for affluence and security is this loss of vitality and confidence.

Fr. Tony Stevens-Arroyo felt that the American bishops lack a sense of what it means to be the American church. An authentic church movement today must be a people-movement. Not until the Latino and Hispanic presence in the U.S. put on boots and marched to change consciousness did the U.S. church seem to know the Spanish-speaking church existed or had needs. Contrary to popular opinion, in such cases, he said, changes are made from outside the system, not within. He gave as an example that when the Hispanics were relating to quotas, to Chavez and the Farmworkers' right to organize, newspapers became interested in Hispanic Catholics. They preferred to interview an involved Mexican-American priest ordained four years rather than the chancery official in charge of migrant ministry. Unlike the African and South American bishops who in disproportion to their numbers have clout and know what "to be Church" means in a political arena, the American bishops seem to lack this kind of awareness, and fall back upon models of machine and ethnic politics.

Catholic Liberalism

Dr. O'Brien pointed out that the dream of the nineteenth century Americanists was of a unified hierarchy, the development of national lay organizations, and a truly national Catholic University which would mobilize the resources of the American church for the mission of the church in the new era. One of the things that died in the 50s and 60s was American Catholic liberalism. It had envisioned a time when the Church, growing beyond its identification solely with ethnicity and minority groups, would enter into the American mainstream and bring about the creation of a new American Catholic culture.

Why did American Catholic liberalism die? Its key moral focus was the belief in the American possibility, that a new era was emerging in history and that America was the key to it—almost a kind of manifest destiny. That spirit carried into the 60s and dominated the initial response to Vatican II. But when the Catonsville Nine went to trial, the defendants stated that they had taken the actions they did because they had learned that the American dream was a lie. They saw their country engaged in an unjustifiable and dishonorable war, refusing to disengage itself for fear of losing face regardless of the cost in thousands of lives on both sides. While they were in a tiny minority, this loss of confidence in America was widespread.

Dr. O'Brien concluded, "I think that is where Catholic liberalism ended, but I think we have to revive it. There aren't many Catholics left who believe that America contains the resources to build a distinctive, energetic, vital, and specifically American Catholicism. But nostalgia alone won't work. We have to revive the sense of possibility.''

Fr. Stevens-Arroyo stated that while the ethnic revival could be nothing more than nostalgia, it could also be an assertion of pluralism and be part of the redefinition of America. But it cannot be just cultural or political pluralism; it must also be economic. In New York, for example, the political, economic, and social situation depends upon jobs, work, money, and services, without which it is ridiculous to talk about more rights, more day care centers, more schools, and so on. He believes that American Catholic liberalism died with American liberalism. A new sense of pluralism is going to resurrect what the American church is all about.

Catholic Radicals

Mrs. Newland recalled that during the years of struggle over the Viet Nam war, her own children were not convinced that she really belonged to the same group that was locally recognized as "the Catholic Church." The Catholics her children admired and identified with were those few whose courage and forthrightness in protesting the war had eventually landed them in trouble and outside the pale of the local parish—which is the "Catholic Church" most young people experience. Their evaluation of their family's stand was that it was radical—but not radically Catholic—and that the people who shared such convictions with them were not representative examples of Catholicism but exceptions to the rule.

Fr. Stevens-Arroyo pondered what it might have been like if the bishops had been able to move away from the war in Viet Nam with the kind of support and solidarity they possessed in the 1880s. "Imagine, in terms of U.S. politics, what the impact of that would have been, a stand which said 'This is what American Catholics are about—U.S. citizens but with a difference.' " He felt such a stand would and could happen—but not just through good will. Concrete action must be taken.

The Gap Between Theology and the People

Dr. Monika Hellwig felt differences in views spring from the fact that while theologians and social action people are concerned with the very life of the church, the populace identifies itself as Catholic on the basis of "going to church." The word *religion,* she pointed out, tends to be attached to people who are regular worshippers, to whom the church is "home" in a sense, a place where their need to belong is fulfilled in a special way. This explains the bewilderment, even anger and opposition, which church-goers show toward those who would change the Church.

Many times reformers, whether liturgists, social action people or theologians, share a suspiciously broad base with the secular humanists in their concern for certain causes, thus losing their religious identification in the popular mind. The tension such differences creates has to be dealt with and resolved if possible, and on the local level such tension usually has to do with very concrete problems. Yet it is impossible to give merely theoretical answers to such questions, because each problem is unique.

The Confirmation Controversy

To illustrate such a difference on the theological level, Dr. Hellwig referred to a problem raised by one of the Religious Education Directors in the Diocese of Albany. The Director had refused to allow a boy who did not fulfill even the minimal requirements set up by the parish and the diocese to be confirmed. The boy's sister accused both the Director and the Church of feigning concern for youth, then pushing this boy away from the sacrament. The Director's question was: "How much does one judge? What standard do we take? Where do we draw the line?" She was caught between a sober theological view of Confirmation and the popular teaching that one should "get the graces."

Dr. Hellwig could sympathize with both the boy and the educator, but as a theologian she felt that it would be unfortunate to distort the meaning of Confirmation by having no requirements for its reception. Infant Baptism requires no commitment on the part of the child, so Confirmation, as it is presently perceived in the Church at the moment, is the classic opportunity to make a commitment. The answer to whom should be confirmed has to be based on prudential judgment, however, since there is no black and white position upon which a right or wrong answer is given. The more difficult question is—what is to be asked for in the way of commitment?

Fr. Stevens-Arroyo approached this problem as an activist and said that Confirmation is a sacrament which calls people to accept responsibility not only as mature individuals committed to the Church, but actually committed to others. Fr. Murnion thought there was considerable question as to the religious commitment that could be significantly made at the eighth grade level. He felt the more pressing need is to find a way to get people to declare themselves about the meaning of their membership in the Church—whether at Confirmation, or as parents at the baptizing of their infants.

Baptismal Preparation

As examples relating to the sacraments were discussed, it became obvious that there was a great gap between theory and practice. Fr. Murnion spoke of a survey done in fifty New York parishes to find out what people thought about Baptism. A number of priests were disturbed about being questioned regarding their own understanding of Baptism. Nonetheless there was considerable difference, he said, about the meaning of Baptism and about the meaning of the Christian community to which it gives entree, and there seemed to be no connection between the meaning of the sacrament and the appropriate preparation for it.

In response to the survey a proposed policy for the archdiocese was developed, which said that the parent of a child to be baptized should give evidence of attempting to meet the minimal standards of what it means to be a Catholic. These minimal standards were: have some idea of what was commonly believed (the Creed), to know the Lord's prayer, to participate in the Eucharist, to practice personal prayer, to have concern for one's neighbor, and to recognize the obligation to correct unjust attitudes. Also, to give some evidence that their children would be supported in their faith life. The policy suggested discussion between an interviewer and the parent(s), with an opportunity to examine the questions together, and provision for instruction based on the needs. The people were not to be interrogated, but rather informed about these minimum requirements, and the instructors were to put their emphasis on the exploring of responsibilities, rather than on questioning to see if the people measured up to these minimum requirements. Admittedly this is a difficult policy when a parish schedules many baptisms per year.

The proposal was circulated throughout the archdiocese for reaction. There was general agreement about the need to say something, although there was some fear that the approach was a bit legalistic. There was great indecision, however, about the difference between the theological and popular conception of sacraments. The question most commonly asked was, "Whatever happened to Limbo?" because the policy suggested postponing Baptism until the sacrament is properly understood.

The problem, Fr. Murnion pointed out, is that the new Rite, while saying a lot about what it means to be a Catholic, leads to more demanding conditions for Baptism. The popular view has emphasized things to be believed about the Catholic Church, rather than personal commitment. This was evident by people's opposition to questions on charity and unjust attitudes. It was asked, "What right does the priest have to pry into my personal life like that?" The popular understanding of the relation between the priest and the people was revealing. He seemed to be a kind of respected factotum but was not expected to bear down on the meaning of the Gospels.

The gap between the theological view of the Christian life and what is popularly understood is wide and crucial. The new Rite for Baptism faces both people and clergy with questions they have no way of handling. Not

Rev. Philip Murnion

only does its emphasis on the baptism of adults make more demands, but the theological and contextual development which produced the Rite came from the liturgists, and was not remotely related to the understanding of most of the congregation or even some of the clergy. Nor is the popular position entirely culpable, since for centuries people learned what they were taught about Baptism and faithfully handed it down. They learned their lessons well and one can appreciate their bewilderment and even anger at having the scene change so dramatically.

Fr. Murnion questioned how fair it was to create new demands for the parents of the about-to-be-baptized while leaving the rest of the congregation untouched by the same demands? Unless the entire community is made aware of the things which are minimal standards for "being Catholic," it becomes a matter of holding the unbaptized children hostage until at least their parents can be made aware of gospel responsibilities.

Gertrude Morris felt that it was an alarming paradox that Catholics would reject social concern as necessary for baptismal preparation. The Last Judgment is described by Christ as a matter of "Whatever you do to even the least of these my brothers. . . ." She cited a survey of converts which revealed that it was neither ritual nor the teaching of the Church which attracted them to Catholicism, but a specific Catholic who was a true Christian, who gave witness to just such concern for charity and justice.

Preparing for Eucharist

In reference to those who value the experiential view of the sacraments as contrasted to those who opt for lists of requirements, Fr. Robley Whitson pointed out that St. Pius X established only two conditions for early Communion—that the recipient have some notion of God, and that this kind of eating is not like other eating. (He also did not require that the child to whom he gave Eucharist at such a tender age go to Confession.) The sacramental experience was to come first, and Pius X, "a reactionary intellectual if there ever was one," said that the direct involvement in the immediate sacramental experience was the germinal experience, without which faith means nothing in the literal sense.

To John Wesley, the reality of Christ present in the Eucharist was crucial and he made a radical innovation of daily Communion. He went into the London prisons and gave Communion to people because, he said, "If Christ truly is the Eucharistic reality, how can I keep him from men who reach out to him?" He was quite aware that such people knew little, and had no way to change their lives, but he presumed that the mere fact that a person reached out was precisely what Jesus himself had responded to in his public ministry. This, Fr. Whitson felt, is a Catholic attitude in the best sense of the word—experience coming first even if nothing else can come. Wesley held that the issue of reverence rested with the priest, not with the one who was incapable of reverence.

People have to be encouraged to be more articulate about what they believe, Dr. O'Brien felt, to discuss publicly why they think it important to be married as a Catholic, to be baptized, and so forth. If the Church is to survive, people must bring to the surface their feelings and convictions about membership, and learn from each others' experiences.

The American Church and Minorities

Father Stevens-Arroyo felt that in the near future the American church is going to have to face the problems the Hispanic church has had to deal with over the past five or six years—problems such as capitalism and social justice. He also felt that the divisions which separate people within the Church's own structure must disappear. Theologically oriented people can no longer remain aloof from social action people and vice versa. The latter will have to be less scornful of the people whose interest in activism is marginal. Such groups working together is Catholicism, he insisted, and as the theologians became more activist and the activists more theological, the people themselves more concerned with both, the process becomes pluralist and can begin to weld together.

Asked what the Church might be like when its majority is eventually Spanish-speaking, Fr. Stevens-Arroyo said the largest number of Catholics in the world today are Hispanic, yet the Church is still very European, very Roman. Aside from all church suppers serving tacos, his guess was that a Hispanic majority would not make a big difference. Something might happen, however, in the relationship of the people to the clergy. In the Hispanic community the clergy have to identify with the people, he said, and used as his example Bishop Flores in the Southwest. "If he's not singing and dancing and eating with them, he's not going to be able to mobilize them afterwards. If he's not going to be with them, they are not going to be with him."

It is a matter of style, he believes, and the question is whether the Hispanics are going to alter the style or the structure, or whether it is going to alter them. He pointed out that there are some Hispanic priests driving big cars, wearing expensive clothes, and looking for nice parishes, because they think that is the way to become the next Spanish-speaking bishop. But with the emergence of the Padres (a group of priests who are active in ministry to the Spanish-speaking) more and more the conviction is that such men will not make the kind of bishops that are needed. Bishops will be chosen from those who are socially involved.

Rev. Antonio Stevens—Arroyo, C.P.

Fr. Stevens-Arroyo stated that if the American church is to become credible to the Latinos, the hierarchy will have to take the Spanish-speaking seriously. The Hispanic church, he held, has emerged out of a sense of desparation and the struggle of the other minority groups for justice. The Latinos have brought the other America into North American Catholicism in the form of Latin culture and the theology of liberation. Born with a theology that had been nurtured by pastoral practice, music, and customs, when they finally came to articulate their identity Hispanics did so in terms of contemporary notions, as well as their rich cultural heritage which they intend to keep. He sees a cohesiveness and influence of the Hispanic church on a nationwide level that is extraordinary, considering what such cohesiveness has accomplished in only five or six years. In 1972, there was a single national office relating to migrant work, with regional offices in Michigan, San Antonio, and California. Now the problem of the migrant workers has been allocated a desk at the USCC. Latino clout at the Call to Action meeting in Detroit was remarkable, especially since the Hispanic stereotype was so difficult to overcome. Hispanic people in the past were supposed to be lazy, manana-type people, but in Detroit quite plainly they were not. Indeed, there they were suspected of being plotting revolutionaries, Che Guevara-types trying to take over. There is a change, and it is from within, and the Hispanics are making it happen themselves.

Unfortunately in the Northeast the Puerto Rican situation has not grown and developed the way the Mexican-American situation has in the Southwest. There the "new Irish" are going to be the Mexican-Americans in whom there is a real sense of messianism.

Some say that soon it will be their turn "to run the church," but it is important to realize that the two experiences—the immigrant and the Latin-American—are not comparable. The latter were here already, and after eleven generations they still have not lost their desire to keep their language alive or their identity distinct.

The Northeast and the Puerto Rican Experience

The grave danger, he continued, is the possibility that in the Northeast large numbers of Puerto Ricans in the Bronx and Manhattan who have been members of the Church, even a kind of backbone of the Church in their areas, might simply say, "We quit." Why? Because their needs have gone unattended. If and when they become militants, they may become secularly militant. About half the advocates of Puerto Rican Independence, both in New York and Puerto Rico, are Catholics who were first involved in community work with the Church. These are people who were moving towards a definition of Christian social democracy for Puerto Rico and found the accomplishment of that goal impossible under U.S. domination. In Puerto Rico, however, there is extreme polarization at present. Catholics either favor the status quo and a conservative church remaining uninvolved, or move over to the Marxist-Leninist movement which at least seems to be on the side of social democracy and the poor. Ironically, one of the members of the central committee for the Puerto Rican Socialist Party is a former seminarian from the Archdiocese of New York.

Fr. Stevens-Arroyo said that one can debate with a Puerto Rican Marxist about atheism, and when the discussion is over, one's adversary might ask, "Will you come and baptize my baby next Sunday?" Why?

He will say he is doing it for his family—although one feels there is a little "Just in case!" mixed in also.

The Puerto Rican experience is very different from the Mexican-American experience, he said, and they do not handle their problems the same way. Puerto Rican identity, for instance, is more a political than a cultural problem. In Puerto Rico, the island is small and the communities close in contrast to the Southwest's wide open spaces: he felt that change in political status is coming rapidly and suspects that the New York church has as much to say about the solution to the problem as the church in Puerto Rico. The latter, Fr. Stevens-Arroyo said, has built a wall between itself and these movements, while in New York that is not true. The Puerto Rican is more conscious of being Puerto Rican in New York than in Puerto Rico.

That the Cardinal of New York should listen to the Hispanic leadership is not just a matter of tact and fair play, but of realizing that Hispanic perception of the struggle for survival in the northeast is the experience of the Church itself. These people *are* the Church and unless this reality is recognized and given voice, there is going to be an emptiness and barrenness in the Church's self-understanding. People of good will who empathize with and participate in the struggle still cannot be authentic voices for disclosing it to others if it is not a part of their life situation.

Fr. Stevens-Arroyo perceives that the question of minorities is a matter of theology as much as of sociology. If the answer to what it means to be a Catholic is to respond to concrete needs of people, then every single step, every support given and advocacy undertaken for these people say, "This is what it means to be a Catholic."

He sees the minorities and ethnic groups as bearers of revelation for the whole Christian community. Instead of viewing the present situation of the Church as a problem that poses such questions as, "What can be done to keep the institution alive? To please its clientele? To heed the hierarchy? To 'market our product,' " minorities call us to another vision. We have to see in their experience—their suffering, oppression, and struggle to find a better way of life—the face of Christ who identified himself with such as these. We have to see how God is present in their lives, their community, and how the Holy Spirit is present in their struggle.

Catholicism and Black Culture

Gertrude Morris, addressing the concern of the Church for the black community, felt that the word *unchurched* does not apply to black people who may be denominationally uninvolved. It certainly does not apply to their religiousness or relation to God. She repeated her conviction that authentic conversions are a result of authentic witness, and maintained that until the Church looks attractive to blacks, these people will remain unmoved by it. The most recent example of this indifference was the Boston experience, where it became apparent that black children were not welcome in schools whose population was predominantly white Catholics.

She pointed out that, ironically, black Catholics would be in a good position to mediate when there are black-white problems because the Catholic community is usually one-sidedly white. The white Catholic community seems unaware that blacks are also in the community. Ms. Morris declared: "We become more black and less Catholic right away when the problems arise." It is preposterous to think about asking blacks in Boston to come to a Catholic church when they have seen the Catholics throwing stones at their children.

Ms. Morris asserted that one of the most important things American Catholics need to learn is that *catholic* with a small *c* means universal and that many of the things we take as religious principles are merely cultural, European, and no more orthodox than the products of any other culture. For example, authentic music has always come out of the people but due to ignorance of this fact, much liturgical music that has come out of black people has been objected to because "It isn't sacred." She pointed out that *O Sacred Head Surrounded* was originally a drinking song.

Blacks complain that many of their pastors don't appreciate black culture. There are slightly more than two hundred black priests in the U.S., so the majority of black Catholics are under white pastors. When, as an American, one goes to a foreign country, one expects to adapt to the country and not to treat the people as though they are the foreigners. This is not how many white priests behave in the black community. They are able to be present in a black parish for twenty years and never take on the richness their constituents have to offer. Not only do they resist influence, they actually try to "whiten" the black people to whom they minister.

The consequence is that there are a lot of black Catholics who go to Mass on Sunday morning and "go to church" in the afternoon, that is, some place where they can sing and be themselves. What people have to realize about black spirituality, Ms. Morris insisted, is that there is a strong sense of "He walks with me and he talks with me." a sense of Christ-with-us, and that the liturgy has to give one the strength to make it through the rest of the week. If such strength is not to be found at the liturgy, one goes where it is to be found, because without it a lot of black people could never get through the week.

She commented that it had taken her years to realize that enjoying church was alien to many Catholics. It is no accident, she pointed out, that many black leaders are also ministers. There is not the division between the secular and the religious for the black community. Without God, the black community could never survive what it has to put up with. There has to be an end to the attitude among American Catholics that "lets the poor blacks do their thing." There must be an awareness that what the black culture has to offer will

Ms. Gertrude Morris stated that there has to be an end to the attitude among American Catholics that "lets the poor blacks do their thing." There must be an awareness that what the black culture has to offer will enrich Catholicism and the religious experience of American Catholics.

enrich Catholicism and the religious experience of American Catholics.

Dr. Monika Hellwig felt that among the things that have emerged out of different contributions of the minorities was a corrective to American activism. The black community, she suggested, offers what one might call the hasidism among the Catholic community, being the ones for whom contemplation and mysticism is not a rare gift but rather a community gift which the wider community needs to have passed on to it. The element of enjoyment which she found rooted in Catholic Europe wherever there is peasant Catholicism, is found in the community that does not depend upon what the priest tells the congregation in church. Rather, it is based on family life-style, is passed on by family life patterns, and where she found this community, not only was worship an enjoyment, but Sunday was a day to be looked forward to, a day of true celebration.

Seminaries, the Religious Life and the Black Experience

David O'Brien felt that another step toward credibility for the Church would be concern for proper preparation in the seminaries and religious communities of the people who will serve the ethnic and minority groups. Ms. Morris agreed and added that the experience of blacks in religious orders and seminaries has been painful and frustrating. She told of a black religious she knew who had been kept from ordination because his community was convinced he could not keep their Rule. He persisted and in time was ordained, and his very presence as a black enriched the community by their own admission. It was a richness they had denied themselves.

Black Leadership

The Church in America must support the leadership of the people in the minority communities if it is to become credible, Fr. Murnion stated, and not only their leadership in the church community but in the society at large, so they can be recognized as black and Catholic, Puerto Rican and Catholic. At the moment, he said parish councils (originally projected as places where leadership might develop) are almost nonexistent in black and Puerto Rican parishes. Just as important is the fact that one concept or pattern for parish councils is unrealistic, since the same structure will not work for each parish. There have to be different ways to establish ownership, not just along ethnic-minority lines but in terms of parish situations in general.

Ms. Morris agreed and commented that where there are community leaders, they are not the polite blacks in the three-piece suits on TV, but are the ones that the community recognizes as leader. The authentic black leader may not look like one but he or she (and very often it is a woman) is followed, listened to, is vital to the community. Such a leader may not be able to articulate a five year plan, but could reflect the community's needs. The black community will tell the white community who its leaders are, not vice versa.

Nor should there be any attempt to enter the black community and exert any form of control, she said. If a group wants to help, the leader should be asked what help is needed, and be humble enough to follow the suggestions—simply because white people do not know the black situation. Many groups who have ignored this procedure have been turned off trying to help in the black community. An example, she cited was a group which wanted to go into the Bedford-Stuyvesant section of Brooklyn and do a clean-up job, much like the highly publicized Harlem event several years ago. But the blacks in Bedford-Stuyvesant did not want a clean-up job. They wanted some white people to do a comparative price check for them in one of the local supermarkets, which was gouging blacks with prices far higher than they charged whites in other sections of the city. But the whites refused. Why? she was asked. "The supposition was that it did not present as exciting or public an opportunity 'to do good', one that might attract the TV cameras."

part two:
Discussion Questions

1. Who is Jesus for You? How do you see the Church as being an expression of Jesus to the world?

2. The participants claim that when life is easy, people do not have a sense of urgency or vitality about being Church. How is this attitude demonstrated by all Church members—from local parishoners to the heirarchy?

3. What are your images of God? of sin? of the Church?

4. Discuss the "gap between theology and people." Use examples from your own experience.

5. What issues would you cite as specifically American Catholic needs?

6. Do you agree with Dr. O'Brien that American Catholic liberalism is dead?

7. Do you believe that Catholics have a "bad press" in America? How would you describe the media image of Catholics? How do you think this image affects people whose only contact with Catholics is through the media?

part three:

ANSWERING THE QUESTION

Pluralism in the Church

Research done on the genetic neurological differences between different groups, Fr. Robley Whitson pointed out, is particularly valuable in an examination of the racial, ethnic, and economic differences. For example, at a tribal ceremony some Indians may sit stolidly for hours without participating physically in dance, while others may never cease to dance. There are all kinds of differences in people about which we are not aware but ought to be, because ignorance of them contributes to stereotyping, bigotry, and oppression. (This posed, he observed, more diocesan problems, such as new offices to serve the stolid.) He continued by pointing out that we spoke of the Church as It for centuries, then Vatican II gave us an image of People rather then It, Us not She, We. In the "*We* church," he said, the first need is to boldly accept the fact that we are a mixed bag, with all sorts of people belonging. If we can stop being blind to this diversity, we can put an end to making incredible errors regarding the differences among us.

The Role of Minorities in the Building Up of the Church

Dr. O'Brien pointed out that it is important to understand that the Church in this country developed most vigorously from the bottom up. The Irish, the Polish, the French Canadians, the Italians literally built the churches themselves. Bishops did not build the churches for them. Similarly, since Vatican II the most vigorous renewal is taking place from the bottom up. Instead of bishops and professionals running around renewing the Church, small groups are doing it. These groups have to be encouraged to come together on the local level to determine their needs, articulate their experience, seek resources to meet the needs from the wider community if necessary. This renewal was stressed in the recommendations of the Call to Action, which reflected a sense of ownership in the community itself.

However, Dr. O'Brien cautioned, the bottom-up approach to minority-ethnic problems alone will not work. It has to be all across the line, in terms of suburbs, city, community, if there is going to be identification of the church with the issues of the people. He proposed a counterpart, a process of community organizing where people are able to take ownership in situations where the common need does cut across ethnic and minority lines. This calls for enormous change in such things as pastoral practice, with radical consequences in such a large institutional Church.

When the black and Hispanic groups come up with their lists of priorities at the Call to Action, seven of the ten were the same issues everybody else had listed—families, schools, and neighborhood development. A massive lack of communication in the Church prejudices the issues. All sorts of people are simply trying to raise their children decently, and in their struggle they are asking the Church for support in getting what is rightly and justly theirs. The goal of the groups we call minority, ethnic, alternate life-style, is not something exotic or different. They are simply people who are seeking the same things other families are looking for—a church setting that meets their needs and gives them support and affirmation.

Dr. O'Brien observed that do-gooders in the Church often ask "What can we do for others?" and yet do not give adequate attention to their own local situation. Sometimes it is easier to get involved in social ministry than to deal with the local parish. He has gone to national meetings, Dr. O'Brien said, and come home to tell his wife what is going on, and she has said, "Yes, but what about our own parish?"

When the question is, "What can active, interested, renewed Catholics do?" his answer is that they continue to do what they do best, struggle to renew the church where they are, make their own community vital and alive. They can keep people growing and open, understanding what it means to be the People of God and heir to this tradition. If we can develop a sense of the mission of the Church at the local level, we will begin to witness to a Church that will be attractive to others, that will lead to articulation of the Church in terms of the broader social, cultural, and human rights problems. The best way for the Church to contribute to liberty and justice is to struggle to be Church—the rest will follow.

Ecumenism and Catholic
Self-Identity

Dr. Monika Hellwig felt that there is ecumenical progress—but not a significant amount of it at the institutional level. Many lay people are deeply involved with non-Catholics in prayer and action groups, but are uninterested in institutional forms of ecumenism or discussions about what makes the churches different. We have always said that God is welcoming, is the single horizon, is gracious, calls us to common destiny. She finds it gratifying that we can now accept that God reveals himself to other people in other ways. Thus we are freer to deal with the problems that separated us and create a confluence of denominational communities. But the Catholic Church she would like to see has not happened yet. We are not truly Catholic, she believes, until we mend schisms with other groups and start sharing our common Christian purpose.

Fr. Stevens-Arroyo sees the difference between Catholic and Christian crystalizing different elements in society. It is interesting to hear how people use the two words Christian and Catholic. Those who want the conservative strategy in order to preserve the institutions are emphasizing that they are *Catolicos*. Those who are concerned that the church identify with the radical movements call themselves *Cristianos*. The *Catolicos* would not say that they are not *Cristianos* but they want to preserve the institutions with the marks and signs of the past. Those who call themselves *Cristianos* say that the difference between Catholics, Methodist, Lutherans, all the rest, is minimal—we are all Christians. In Latin America, he believes, if this movement toward liberation continues, there will be persecution.

Fr. Stevens-Arroyo feels that a growing number of people in North America no longer feel attracted to the institutional Church. After trying for a number of years, they do not have the energy left to spend convincing pre-Vatican II pastors that a renewed vision is good, vital, crucial. The danger, he felt, is that the meaning of *Catholic* will become so identified with cautiousness and conservatism that ever greater fragmentation will result, and the Church will be left with little influence.

The goal of ecumenism seems to him to be not so much the merging of different confessions, as a reshuffling of those who wish to unify themselves in terms of the practice of Christian love and service. Minimizing the things which otherwise have separated them, such a group may prefer to identify themselves for that very reason as Christian. Those who do not want to go that route, he feels, could continue to keep their separate denominational names—Catholic, Lutheran, Episcopalians.

Middle-Class Ecumenism

Ecumenism among the middle class people in the large Chicago area, Father David Murphy felt, is best characterized by a kind of tolerance or sense of indifference, not because Catholics look down on Protestants but because they have the same attitude towards their own religion. The spirit is reflected in the attitude of the college students he sees when they frankly admit, "We're all the same." It is not said in any spirit of real interest in the problem but rather with a kind of blase attitude which they have come to by themselves, or from going to school with members of other denominations, or from their own ignorance of or indifference to their Catholic teaching.

Fr. Murphy wonders if there are not a lot of people out there who are never "coming back." He is concerned about young adults who for whatever reason have disassociated themselves from the Church. Church attendance aside, he has noticed that they have little appreciation for things sacramental, are caught up with consumerism and its measures of success, and they become angry with the Church when it impinges on the kind of life they want to lead. They have adopted what we may call the "new theology" but which they think allows them to make up their minds about anything they want to do. Fr. Murphy felt that this group comprises another kind of drop-out. They may enjoy specific liturgies, but they are able to insulate their lives so that they can get along without what it is that the post-Vatican II reformers are trying to do. He felt a certain envy for Fr. Stevens-Arroyo because the group he works with are at least concerned. It is infinitely more difficult to work with people who do not seem to care.

Rev. David Murphy, O.Carm.

Other Ecumenical Dimensions

Fr. Robley Whitson pointed out that the impact of various separated Christians conversing about their differences is not going to be forgotten so easily, although one may not know at the moment what it ultimately signifies. It could be merely superficial, like collecting old buddha statues to put flowers in. Or it might be speaking to us of another set of dimensions that will wake us up. It certainly moves us away from parochialism to a world view of religion.

Fr. Whitson felt that at the end of the Council there was extreme naivetee which emotionally defined ecumenism as inter-institutional, and which produced great negotiations among ecclestiastics, theologians, and so forth, as well as a lot of good information. But that is not what ecumenism is all about. What is at stake is the need to realize that Christian bodies of people represent a tremendous diversity, not just in terms of liturgy, doctrines, and styles of practice, but in the approach to the vital questions. His own experience with the Shakers, for instance, has shown him the phenomenon of a numerically tiny church dying out which is not clinging to life, and takes for granted that all institutions are as mortal as the mortals who make them up. Mother Ann, the foundress of the Shakers, said, "If there is only one who is faithful in a generation, that is enough because the world is saved by generations." The Shakers have a sense of community which teaches that even if the life-giving process is reduced to one person, the capacity to generate life is centered in the person (rather than in organizational institutions). A single individual can embody a community.

As one who is thoroughly Catholic as well as Shaker, Fr. Whitson feels no contradictions in his loyalties. He believes that first and most basic is the fact that underneath, all our human experience is common and shared. If one perceives the reality of that experience, the question arises, "What does it mean?" and sharing the question and search for answers is more than empathy with individuals, or with other groups. Such "ecumenical" sharing can enlarge our self-identity, and may reveal, as his experience with the Shakers has revealed to him, that we can truly identify with others. He feels that this perception of shared experience is a process which is actually going on in the world, that our self-consciousness is expanding, that we are growing in a new way.

What is called for, he feels, is a reformation of attitude rather than of institutional procedures or a convergence of theologies. The groups who are likely to give us this kind of enrichment from their insights, so different from our own, are often those who are farthest removed from us.

Movements Bridge
Denominations

Dr. O'Brien felt that the next generation of movements would see a multiplication of groups like the charismatic movement, Marriage Encounter, and so forth. Young adults and older people alike are coming together around common interests and concerns. Such movements will in time change denominational divisions. In the past there have already been intrachurch tensions created by what has been called the two-party system'' within the Christian denominations—social gospel people vs. pietism people, modernists vs. fundamentalists, and so on. He felt the same would happen in parishes where liberal and conservative sides emerge. In time, however, a commonality will develop between Catholics and Protestants who share the same concerns. If the Catholic Church is wise and adheres to its best tradition of allowing room for many such positions, it could become a kind of umbrella for such activity.

Gertrude Morris felt that this commonality is already happening around issues such as ecology, political corruption, and hunger. People cut across lines because they get involved in an issue. Becoming concerned, caring, they become more themselves. David O'Brien pointed out that in New England there are already a significant number of alternative communities of young people interested in the energy question, the nuclear power issues, and other topics. Interestingly enough, he said, there is a significant response to these groups on campuses where young people are talking to each other in down to earth ways. He felt that if the tax credit bill had gone through, there would have been a revival of alternative schools, especially with so many unemployed frustrated teachers around. There is tremendous discontent in the schools, he claimed, and when people are frustrated the grounds for social protest and revolution are riper than for simple oppression.

Social Issues and Young People

Dr. O'Brien felt that generosity and compassion were very real among college students and hoped that if a crisis should emerge, either socially or in their own lives, they would hold to those values. His hope would be that the Church would respond. The reason the Clam Shell Alliance* and other such communities are important is that they at least are trying to articulate reasonable response to a situation that needs one. It may be that like the peace movement, which was so small in the 50s and arrived in the 60s, the significant protest in the 80s will come out of these groups.

The importance of involvement with social service is crucial, Dr. O'Brien believed. Even if they are not going to change the society, the involvement of young people with others in need develops an awareness that there are really such people who have needs through no fault of their own. Ms. Morris added that even if they go into it for the wrong reasons, the experience itself changes them.

A resurgence of the kinds of movements and demonstrations seen in the 60s is a real possibility for

---

*The Clam Shell Alliance is an anti-nuclear reactor protest group, founded in 1976, whose members work to unite anti-nuclear forces, to educate people to the dangers of nuclear power, and to publicize military subsidies of nuclear research.

the 80s, Fr. Murnion felt, because the problems remain and are even more severe at present. They could be exacerbated by growing unemployment, energy cuts, and so on, and begin to affect at least the people in the cities who not only think they have nothing to lose but that there is nothing to win. They will express their rage now—because they have ten or fifteen years of experience seeing rage expressed. These movements will test the churches seriously and will multiply the number of churches that will be divided along not only class lines but also ideological lines. The degree to which the Catholic Church tries to embrace the problem will determine whether it can maintain any degree of universality.

He commented that a survey done in the *Christian Science Monitor* about city neighborhoods revealed that when people were asked what institutions were doing the most to try to help the neighborhoods, the churches were most often cited. It was interesting that people saw the Church as an important resource in the recovery of the neighborhoods, whatever their obvious disaffection for the Church. The danger would be that rather than be harnessed for such an effort, the growing fragmentation of the churches would polarize them and they would become part of the larger left-right division in society.

part three:
Discussion Questions

1. How do you think a sense of mission can be developed in the Church on the local level?

2. How do you think commonality can best be encouraged?

3. Fr. Stevens-Arroyo commented on the popular differences between being identified as *Catholic* and *Christian*. What differences between the two terms are there in your mind? If someone you knew preferred to be called a *Christian* rather than a Catholic, what questions would you ask that person about that preference?

4. What do you think Fr. Murphy meant by the term "new theology"? Who do you think has adopted this new attitude and way of thinking?

5. There exists now in the Church tensions created by the "two-party system." What is meant by the term, and where do you see this system leading the Church in the years ahead?

6. What place does critical self-analysis and self-questioning have in your faith? Do you feel it is a beneficial or a damaging attitude toward faith?

7. How would you personally respond to the question, Why be a Catholic?

part four:
SUMMARY

The final discussion of the Forum was devoted to a personal response to the question, "Why be a Catholic?" Gertrude Morris said that there were many answers she might give, but that paramount at the moment was her delight that such a gathering could take place and that a group of Catholics could come together to ask "why"? She was grateful that Catholics are free to say deeply critical things about the Church, to face the kinds of faults and failures in the Church which are the most frightening, and not feel disloyal in doing so. Catholics may not always be pleased with what they see in the Church but they can have real hope that what should happen can happen. That for her is another good reason, out of many others, for being a Catholic.

Dr. Monika Hellwig said her reasons are mostly focussed on the totality of Catholicism over the centuries and in all the cultures; for her it is the most coherent way of being a follower of Jesus Christ and of setting about the task of the redemption of the world. She cherishes its rich spiritual tradition and the fact that its broad range of sensibilities cuts across a great variety of cultural and emotional patterns, personal and group constitutions to draw all kinds of people into a non-elitist and intimate communion with Jesus. She sees the Church in an on-going effort to deal with faith in the light of new questions, philosophies, situations, steadfastly refusing to be one with "the world" in order to survive, and remaining separate in order to cope with and to critique the world. She is glad that Catholicism can return to its past and learn from it. If Catholicism has a unique charism, she feels it is "sticking with it." There has been corruption and scandal in the Church in the past, it is true, but the human element in every institution fails from time to time. The Catholic Church, rather than dismantling itself, tries to correct what is wrong and do better in the future.

Fr. Robley Whitson saw the Church as a huge body of people—anybody, everybody, all sorts of people, the good as well as the bad, a community of communities. It does not have a norm only in a Bible, a council, a single tradition, but also in the fact that the entire body is called upon to form a mind—"the mind of the Church." He pointed out that the root meaning of church (ekklesia) is to be "gathered by being called by name," and he noted that it means to be called out of one way of life into another—but this new life is not revealed to us as a "thing." "Being church," is a mystery, and we do not have the easy option of consulting someone's book or someone's abstract principle to discover its meaning. Instead we are left with the struggle to remain open by means of what we call our spirituality, our sense of mysticism, our experience of the sacramental in order to continue to be "the mind of the Church." In answer to the question, "Why be a Catholic?" Fr. Whitson found it eminently worthwhile being part of this body and this process which is focused on revealing the mystery of Christ's Church.

Fr. Philip Murnion enjoys being a Catholic for many reasons, he said, starting with the Church that was communicated to him in his childhood by his family and the priests and sisters who represented Church to him then. They told him of a God who was both demanding and merciful, whose love, even when he sometimes failed it, was constant and forgiving. It is a Church that is more a collective than a single community, where he finds like-minded people as well as many others unlike himself. He can celebrate Mass together with folks from Little Italy and the Bowery, people not living the kind of life he lives nor communicating on the same plane, and yet feel a real sense of family. As an adult Catholic, he has inherited from the Church a stability of commitment to the world, a doggedness, a sense of staying in place which tides him over when there seems no reason to stay.

Working in the Church involves him with institutions dealing with education, health, welfare, families, teenagers, where irresponsibility and abuse have created still more complicated problems. The Church has never said, "We don't have to be worried about that." Rather, it has always said, "We have to be worried about that—but we have to be worried about it in a special way."

The kind of freedom and room for differences to be found in Catholicism was personified for him by his mother when he asked her what she thought of the ordination of women. "I don't think I'd like that," she said. He asked if there were no just reasons for withholding ordination for women, would she still oppose it? She said, "No, They should be ordained. But I won't like it."

Father Murphy's reasons were similar to Dr. Hellwig's and Fr. Murnion's. His own catholicity, he said, is fundamentally based on belief in Jesus Christ who, in turn, has caused a certain restlessness in him that is characteristic of his search or pilgrimage through life. Knowing that nothing is going to satisfy the ego that is probably rampant in him, he said the trust the Lord demands is extremely annoying at times because he would much rather be in control of his life himself. Yet it is because of Christ and the whole Catholic tradition in which he was reared that a flow of love and forgiveness has been opened up to him. He has been given an attitude about life that is purposeful and stable and has offered him frequent times of celebration and joy. To be a Catholic opens up the meaning of what he is trying to do with his life according to his own cultural adaptation. Who he is, Jesus is, and other people are— that is the take-off point. His Catholicism gives him the opportunity to go out and help others and to be concerned.

Father Stevens-Arroyo observed that one has to belong to some community in order to be human and of the communities that exist in the world, the one that is Christian and Catholic has a force and meaning that is real not just to him as an individual, but is historically real for everyone. Belonging to the Church which Jesus began with his life and witness is to belong to a community that both proclaims and practices equality in its fullest meaning. It was the first community in history to say, "From each according to his ability, to each according to his need." It is an international community which has always maintained, even if in fits and starts, a sense of sharing, of sacrifice, of belonging to one another, through its witness of church, religious life, monasticism and the service of the peoples.

It is a community which must be appreciated and renewed. Centered on Jesus, members of the Church must learn to accept others as they must learn to accept themselves. The Catholic tradition with its reconciliation and forgiveness provides renewal and transformation for each of us when we become simultaneously aware of our own smallness and the presence in us of Jesus. He pointed out that as an individual he is a sinner, but belongs to a community which accepts him with all his weakness, and which takes him into its life. He can be a saint—together with all the others whose accumulated goodness can be shared to help build a world that incarnates what Jesus lived and died for. To belong to the Church, he said, is the only way that he can have a sense of permanency, transcendence, transparency, a sense of being gift—that is why he is a Catholic.

David O'Brien said he thought the question would be better put, "Why be an American Catholic?" Why should one try to affirm and live by the promise of our history, the promise of the dignity of the human person, of equality, peace, justice, love? We live at a time when our choice on the question will determine the entire future of our planet, whether we like it or not. Within that frame, the affirmation of Christianity is important because it provides the surest ground for the hope and possibility of a human future. That is the frame, he said, within which he chooses to be Catholic—because its unity, universality, and institutional network make it the most comprehensive source for and contact with the Christian promise and for making that promise live in our times. The Church is the strongest and most available forum and network for resistance to the dehumanizing powers of our time.

Concretely, he is Catholic because he responds to a call which comes, sometimes directly and individually but more often as a gift and task imposed by parents, friends, priests, nuns, other Catholics. It is silly and un-American to imagine that the word of God could be preached and the community of Christian people be present without their own participation and struggle. We have come, as Catholics, from people who moved out across an ocean to a new land, into new worlds where the Gospel was preached only because people insured that it was. It is equally foolish to imagine that the promises of Christianity can be kept alive today without our participation and struggle.

If one wanted to scare people one might quote Sam Adams who spoke (after the Stamp Act crisis), to those dispirited Colonists who were giving up the struggle for American liberty. "If you want to go back and live on your farms and get married and not worry about the struggle, then depart from us in peace, but may posterity forget that you were our countryman." The scenario for the future may be a few Christians sitting around the ruins of an atomic war, or a few Christians sitting around in the midst of an American church with its headquarters and Pope in Cairo, Illinois, posterity will be our judge in some way, and if one wants to get a little worried about our response to the struggle to learn what it means to be an American Catholic, one might think of what posterity will say—and be—if we say "No."

At this point the forum dialogue came to a close. It had become more obvious than ever that there are no simple answers to the question "Why be a Catholic?" Today's Church is far too dynamic and pluralistic to allow for a clear set of reasons for being a member of this community.

Soon after the Forum both Pope Paul VI and Pope John Paul I died. With the election of Pope John Paul II, we feel that an exciting period in the Church has opened, one which will perhaps offer new and challenging reasons for being a Catholic.

SELECTED READING

The following books are also available from the Religious Education Division of the Wm. C. Brown Company Publishers:

Whatever Happened to Good Old Plastic Jesus?

In this sequel to his earlier bestseller, *Good Old Plastic Jesus,* Earnest Larsen explains in free verse his theory of psychotheology.

He combines modern psychological principles and his experiences while working in a drug rehabilitation center. Larsen shows how the intensity of personal feelings and emotions can produce a spiritual awakening. He suggests that the depth of finding God depends on the depth of finding one's own self. (Order #1696, $3.95)

The Ministry Explosion

Ministry, Father Robert Hater maintains, is not restricted to ordained clergy or evangelical Protestants. Ministry is the right and privilege of every baptized Christian.

In this book, Father Hater reviews the how, why, when, and where of ministry today. He calls for recommitment to the work that he feels is the key to self-understanding for individual Christians and the Christian community. (Order #1709, $3.25)

Growing in Faith with Your Child/Creciendo en Fe con Su Nino

This bilingual (English/Spanish) photo booklet directs parents in responding to the basic physical, emotional and spiritual needs of very young children. Having had these needs successfully met, a child will be more open and responsive when formal religious education begins.

The book contains twenty chapters covering a wide range of needs. Each contains a Child's Message with representative photograph, Parent's Response, Adult Reflection and brief Bible Quotation. It is edited by Rev. Thomas P. Ivory and published in cooperation with the Archdiocese of Newark. (Order #1693, $2.00)

Theologians and Catechists in Dialogue: The Albany Forum
In 1977, six experienced catechists and six experienced theologians met to discuss how best to work cooperatively in four areas of common interest. This book, an excellent sourcebook for any religious educator, is a condensation of these discussions. It is expertly edited by Mary Reed Newland and Brennan Hill, Ph.D., both from the Religious Education Office of the Albany Diocese.
Some of the participants in this lively and informative exchange are: Rev. James DiGiacomo, S.J., Dr. Gloria Durka, Rev. Berard Marthaler, O.F.M., Rev. Matthew Lamb, Brother Gabriel Moran, F.S.C., and Bishop Raymond A. Lucker. (Order #1671, $1.85)

IN HIS LIGHT
Using a question-answer approach, Rev. William Anderson, Ph.D. presents current theological thought and trends in non-theological language. In simple terms, Father Anderson explains the traditional concepts of Catholic faith, prayers, and practices. The book is recommended for adults interested in a concise explanation of the faith—and for those preparing for the sacraments of baptism and confirmation. It may also be used as a sourcebook by priests, adult education teachers, discussion groups and as a home library reference. (Order #1716, $4.95)

To order send check or money order to:

Wm. C. Brown Company Publishers
Religious Education Division
2460 Kerper Boulevard
Dubuque, Iowa 52001

—NOTES—

—NOTES—

—NOTES—

—NOTES—

—NOTES—

—NOTES—

—NOTES—

—NOTES—

—NOTES—

—NOTES—

—NOTES—